Little Girls in Church

ALSO BY KATHLEEN NORRIS

Nonfiction

Dakota: A Spiritual Geography, 1993

Poetry Chapbooks

The Astronomy of Love, 1994
All Souls, 1993
How I Came to Drink My Grandmother's Piano, 1989
The Year of Common Things, 1988
From South Dakota, 1978

Poetry

The Middle of the World, 1981
Falling Off, 1971

LITTLE GIRLS IN CHURCH

Kathleen Norris

For
Martha
— PEACE —

Kathleen
Norris

University of Pittsburgh Press
Pittsburgh • London

The publication of this book is supported by grants from the National Endowment for the Arts in Washington, D.C., a Federal agency, and the Pennsylvania Council on the Arts.

Published by the University of Pittsburgh Press, Pittsburgh, Pa. 15260

Library of Congress Cataloging-in-Publication Data

Norris, Kathleen, 1947–
Little girls in church / Kathleen Norris
      p.   cm. —(Pitt Poetry Series)
   ISBN 0-8229-3875-8 (cl.).—ISBN 0-8229-5556-3 (pbk.)
    I. Title.   II. Series.
PS3564.066L58   1995   94-44508
  811'.54—dc20   CIP

A CIP catalogue record for this book is available from the British Library.
Eurospan, London

A detailed list of acknowledgments begins on page 79.

Book Design: Frank Lehner

For David

CONTENTS

LITTLE GIRLS IN CHURCH

A Prayer to Eve

Mother of fictions
and of irony,
help us to laugh.

Mother of science
and the critical method,
keep us humble.

Muse of listeners,
hope of interpreters,
inspire us to act.

Bless our metaphors,
that we might eat them.

Help us to know, Eve,
the one thing we must do.

Come with us, muse of exile,
mother of the road.

POMMES DE TERRE

Three women laugh aloud
in a sun-dappled kitchen
in 1927, in South Dakota.
They are learning French
to improve themselves.

Twice a week they come together:
today, they are naming vegetables.
"*Haricots verts*," one reads aloud,
pointing to the beans. "Green," says Elsa,
the German picture-bride,
lamenting the forests
she will never see again.
Lottie and Myrtle
recall a paradise of their own,
gentle hills at Sioux City, on down
along the river.

They laugh in the afternoon
in a house set down on a God-forsaken,
near-treeless plain.
Each tree they planted in town
either broke with ice
or wilted in the rainless summer.

"*Chou-fleur*," they say,
for cauliflower. Potatoes
are "*pommes de terre*."
The words have such a comforting sound
Lottie repeats them,
like a mother
comforting a child.

Oh, my little earth apples,
little *pommes de terre,*
my cabbage flowers,
oh yes: and now
the womens' cheeks and breasts are blooming,
their bottoms grow round
in the chintz dresses.

They are ladies, yes,
pious and respectable,
but they are laughing now,
beyond caring.

Such elegant potatoes:
pommes de terre, my dear,
oh my dears, oh yes.

KITCHEN TRINITY

Three women
at a table
hold the world.

One gets up
to stir the stars,
one makes the fire,
another blows on it
to keep it going;
and still they have time for play,

three women
hunched over a cup,
hands open in invitation
as the table tilts
in Rublev's icon,

three angels
with the same face.

My mother is the tree trunk I climb,
my grandmother's hands
kneading bread
make the table shake.

Tell me the story
of three hungry angels
who appeared one day at Abraham's tent,
to make Sarah work
and laugh.

PERSEPHONE

I was not a good daughter;
I coveted the cool of dark
after sun-brilliant days,
and dreamed of spiraling to the stars.

He saw me and desired me
and took me to unimagined night.
I was afraid at first
and mourned my sweet flowers.
But I learned to eat
what was put before me,
and became a wife.

My mother raged, my husband
capitulated. When the deal was struck
no one thought I'd be torn in two.

Now I have my pied-à-terre,
and the inner darkness.
Sometimes I think it comes to nothing.

Now spring is a blind green wall.

PERENNIALS

I've betrayed them all:
columbine and daisy,
iris, day-lily,
even the rain barrel
that spoke to me in a dream.

I inherited this garden,
and miss my grandmother
in her big sun hat.
My inexperienced hands
don't know what to hope for.

Still, flowers come; yellow,
pink, and blue. Preoccupied,
I let them go
until weeds produce spikes
and seeds around them.

I never used the rain barrel.
Water froze in the bottom;
too late I set it on its side.

Now lily-of-the-valley comes
with its shy bloom,
choked by a weed
I don't know the name of. One day,
too late, I'll weed around them,
and pull some lilies by mistake.

Next year we'll all be back,
struggling.

Just look at these flowers
I've done nothing to deserve:
and still, they won't abandon me.

THE WEDDING IN THE COURTHOUSE

I don't like weddings.
When you live here
long enough
all the spindly legged girls
grow up like weeds
to be mowed down: matrons
at twenty-five, all edges taken off.
When the music starts
they're led down the aisle
in their white dresses
and we celebrate sentiment
and money.

There's only one wedding
I'd go to again.
I happened to be on an errand
at the county courthouse
and Lucille came running:
"Will you be a witness?
We need two,
and the girls can't leave their desks."

They'd shown up
that morning, no family or friends.
Not kids: he looked about thirty
and she just a little younger.
They couldn't stop smiling.
She may have been pregnant,
but you couldn't tell.
It might have been the denim jumper
she was wearing.

I can picture Lucille
chain-smoking: surprised
and pleased
to interrupt routine.
And the Deputy Sheriff,
a young man, blushing,
loaded gun in his holster,
arms hanging loose.
He looked at his shoes.

It's the words I remember most.
Lucille put out a cigarette
and began: "Dearly beloved,"
and we were!

THE WINE

—for David

I

If you knew how they bored me,
dear, you'd never regret
not being one of my grand passions.

If you knew how cold
was that attention I gave them,
chilled to perfection, like champagne:

how we exhausted ourselves
and grew irritable
or worse,
as it all went flat.

II

We set up battered lawn chairs
on the apartment roof
and sat down to see
how the sun went on.
Across the way a child played at sweeping
while a woman pulled laundry
off a line. It was New York City,
but the air seemed full of spices,
more like Jerusalem
than any town I knew:
the pale red roofs
of the East Village
turning gold,
then blue.

A few stars ventured forth,
a crescent moon between two tenements,
as stars made of wine
exploded on our tongues:
Dominicans and Methodists
singing in the corridors of childhood,
more solemn, in memory,
more in tune.

"We were all once
inside a star," you said,
the ever-faithful scientist.
The noise of the city was as constant as the sea.

III

Fifteen years, driving through another country,
a prairie like the sea
and a sky so full
I know that everything has changed,
you say, "We're looking at the center . . .
we usually see only the stars
on the end of our spiral wing . . . you know,
the Milky Way has two spirals,
kind of like wings . . . "

. . . Like an angel, I am thinking
as we head into the cloud of stars
at the center of our galaxy,
speaking of distant cities
and homemade wine. "All right,"
I say, "I love you."

FOR MY AUNT MARY

Mary, come home.
For too long you've wandered this prairie,
haunted by farm boys
with strong arms
and big, sunburned faces.
We have nothing more to hide.

A photograph spoke to you
in the dust-bound parsonage,
the shaded room that kept the past:
your aunt from West Virginia
modeling a hat
in her millinery store, not at all
proper
for a doctor's wife.
He sold the store;
she had a child
and ran to Baltimore, where the police
found her hoarding netting and feathers.
She'd smothered the baby,
couldn't remember her name . . .

Her story possessed you
as a child. I heard your story
when I was twelve,
and wandered after
your bad endings,
thinking I'd never marry,
settling badly into it
when I did.
When it came time to choose,
I saw my husband clearly

for the first time.
We didn't make a story
for the family to mull over,
a child to grasp
in darkness: your story ended then.

II

Were you a Deborah,
called to battle? Or
a Magdalene, a witness?
You were just a small-town girl,
and no one would listen
or make room. You killed yourself
at the State Hospital
the year I was born,
a few days after you had your baby,
still Jesus' good girl, desperate
for union, for the body's holy
beauty (diagnosis: "promiscuous,"
"talkative," "insight poor").

Even after you died,
your love went on consuming.
I know the hunger's terrible:
I love you, Mary,
I want to bring you rest. What you see
is just the lovers in the garden,
before the Fall.
We both wish them well.
Come away from them now, Mary,
let them be.

HOUSECLEANING

The dreamer descends through the basement to see
what was valuable in her inheritance. —NOR HALL,
THE MOON AND THE VIRGIN

Kneeling in the dust, I recall
the church in Enna, Sicily,
where Ceres and Proserpine reigned
until a pope kicked them out
in the mid-nineteenth century.

This is my Hades, where I find
what the house has eaten.
    And Jessica was left with only
    the raw, sheer, endless terror
    of being alone in the world.
"We are alone, Jessica," I say aloud;
the whole box of romances must go.

I keep the photograph of a young girl
reading cross-legged
under cottonwoods,
her belly still flat, not yet a fruit
split open, the child shining
in its membrane
like a pomegranate seed.

She ended both their lives,
and no mother's rage or weeping
could bring them back.
I leave her with the book of fairy tales:
still safe, held fast,
in Sleeping Beauty's bramble forest.

I could use some sleep.
What I do must be done
each day, in every season,
like liturgy. I pray
to Mary Magdalene, who kept seven demons,
one for each day of the week.
How practical; how womanly.

My barren black cat rubs against my legs.
I think of the barren women
exhorted by the Good Book
to break into song:
we should sing, dear cat,
for the children who will come in our old age.
The cat doesn't laugh,
but I do. She rolls in dust
as I finish sweeping.

I empty the washer
and gather what I need for the return:
the basket of wet clothes
and bag of clothespins,
a worn, spring jacket in need of mending.
Then I head upstairs, singing an old hymn.

THREE WISDOM POEMS

I. LaVonne's Mantlepiece

"Did you know," LaVonne says,
"that schools are teaching Communism,
and not our American way?"
Remember, now, LaVonne's a gentle person,
this is her way of making conversation
in a world full of danger: one sister
a Unitarian, another marrying
a Catholic. "It breaks my heart," she says,
fingering their photographs
on her mantlepiece.
Tonight she wants me to come with her
to a Church of God revival meeting.
"Do I look like I need reviving?" I ask,
and she laughs. But then
she gets her confused look,
and I remember that for all the abuse
LaVonne has taken in her life,
she's the least resentful person I know.
I say, "I guess all these churches
are doing the best they can,"
and LaVonne beams back: "Oh, don't you think
the true church is in the heart?"

II. Physics Defeats Me Once Again, But Wisdom Saves the Day

My sailor friend,
a useful man named Pete,
took me to meet her in a waterfront bar.

We sat in darkness,
away from the neon horseshoe
and I must have looked as stern
as a schoolmarm, because she stood there stark naked
and winked and called out,
"Smile, honey. This is serious."
"Yes," I replied, "I know."

For her finale,
she rotated her breasts
in opposite directions.
"I've always wanted to do that," I told her
when she joined us for a drink.
She looked at me appraisingly.

"You're too small," she said.
But she said it kindly,
and that's what matters.

III. My Favorite Woman in the World

The dogwood tree by the poisoned Susquehanna
is like some women
in love. Breathing in soot,
drinking water as brown
and stinky as shoe polish,
it gives back all it can
of blossom, and heavy with that grace,
bows low before the industrial gods of Harrisburg,
men who know how things are done.

My favorite woman in the world
died sometime in the fifth century.
She loved her husband,
the way some women will,
and built him a monument at Salonae.
Men had told her
how the universe
would settle, this way
or that. How some would burn,
and others find eternal rest.

Look, she loved him and he died.
So, inscribing his tombstone
in bad Latin
while the great Empire crumbled around her,
she reached out
with one impossible gesture,
to protect him from all harm,
and commended him to the mercy
of both Jesus Christ
and the Fates.

In Praise of Darkness

There is, beneath the curved superstructure of every
temple to God-the-father, the dark cave or inner hall
or cellar to Mary, Mere, mut, mutter, *pray for us.*
—H.D., "The Gift"

It does not fall, it rises
out of crevasse and ravine,
to take the hills and mountains,
and then embrace the stars,

calm as the sea-rhythm
in our veins, ancient
and simple as salt.

Think of the eye
forming in the womb: the egg,
the fish, the swimmer.
Think of female matter
that philosophers disdain,
and johns in cheap hotel rooms
fill with money, or themselves,
and fail and fail again
to return to. Think of ladies of the night.

It does not fall, it rises
like a serpent roused from sleep.
It shows itself—a double helix—
in the dream of a geneticist
who translates the code of life.

It simplifies; it breaks all codes,
turning seed into corn, talk
to wisdom, as day unto day

takes up the story, night unto night
the message, without a word . . .

Listen. Be still.
Be as deep as the dark
from which you came. Where we are
is home: only *mut, mutter,* pray for us.

St. Mary of Egypt Speaks to a Gentleman in a Victorian Whorehouse

I recognize this place,
the cheap, red walls;
centuries don't change a whorehouse.
Even in the bonds
you tie me with
I am always perfecting
my love for you,
and you are speechless
in adoration.

It's time for you
to reach for coins,
and if the fancy strikes,
see how many of them
you can stuff in my cunt.

Money protects you,
and the law. I don't have your manners,
just a story
I've carried through the ages:
when you dismember me to find my soul,
I escape into that desert
where you're afraid to go.
I live, and you don't know how.
Give up repeating, this
endless spending and wasting.
You'll never again
have to ask me to die.

THINKING ABOUT LOUISE BOGAN

Alone with Orion—a lesson,
the woman said,
in drawing a straight line—
I'm home. This
is what I fought for,
to draw from the darkness
as from a well.

I endured, she said,
without the gift of faith
and made what I needed
out of work and love and
stolen time. I kept at the writing,
and refused the sacred bowl of broth—
dressed-up Sundays,
china never used,
but weekly dusted.

In this, our city,
a woman might find
good quality of night.
In our spidery house
where ghosts sit weeping
in front of mirrors,
Orion might bend
and hearts love
more fiercely.
Our prayer would read:
give us this day
our daily darkness,
deliver us not
from temptation.

Hester Prynne Recalls a Sunday in June

Our affair had begun,
a sweet time.
I looked forward so to seeing him,
dark figure in sunlight.
When the moment struck—his sermon
drew fire—I saw quite clearly
that he had ritual,
law, the Word,
and I had nothing but myself.

All that
is in the past.
Now respectable women
seek my hand; I must find each broken thread
and make it sing.

They stay and talk now
as I sew. It's as if they expect me
to tell them something,
a secret I brought up
out of chaos.

But I've been too long outside
the comfort they found
in other kingdoms. Pray for me,
I tell them,
if you are my friends.

LITTLE GIRLS IN CHURCH

I

I've made friends
with a five-year-old
Presbyterian. She tugs at her lace collar,
I sympathize. We're both bored.
I give her a pencil;
she draws the moon,
grass, stars, and
I name them for her,
printing in large letters.
The church bulletin
begins to fill.
Carefully, she prints her name
on it, *KATHY,* and hands it back.

Just last week,
in New York City, the Orthodox liturgy
was typically intimate,
casual. An old woman greeted the icons
one by one
and fell asleep
during the Great Litany.
People went in and out,
to smoke cigarettes and chat on the steps.

A girl with long brown braids
was led to the icons
by her mother. They kissed each one,
and the girl made a confession
to the youngest priest. I longed to hear it,
to know her name.

II

I worry for the girls.
I once had braids,
and wore lace that made me suffer.
I had not yet done the things
that would need forgiving.

Church was for singing, and so I sang.
I received a Bible, stars
for all the verses;
I turned and ran.

The music brought me back
from time to time,
singing hymns
in the great breathing body
of a congregation.
And once in Paris, as
I stepped into Notre Dame
to get out of the rain,
the organist began to play:
I stood rooted to the spot,
looked up, and believed.

It didn't last.
Dear girls, my friends,
may you find great love
within you, starlike
and wild, as wide as grass,
solemn as the moon.
I will pray for you, if I can.

THE AGE OF REASON

When I was four, I could draw as well as Raphael.
It has taken me my whole life to learn to draw like a
four-year-old child.—PABLO PICASSO

I

Late one summer evening
we thought you lost
in the ravine
behind the house. You told me once
God cut it in the earth, angry
because people would not love him.

You had built a cocoon of branches
and were curled
inside it, sound asleep.
We broke it open, unfolded you,
and carried you to the house.

After first communion,
I held the veil you handed me
and felt suddenly ashamed
that we'd broken in like that,
the branches too thick,
the entrance too low and narrow
for us to crawl through. And now
you'd seen us
for the fools we were,
celebrating nothing
in the disastrous place we'd brought you to.

II

Now it begins: the search for a God
who has moved on, the
God-please-help-me need
you still can't imagine; strangely
twisted landscapes
in which you may not rest.
The pillar of cloud
you saw march across the plain
will pass you by; some younger child
will see it.

It was given
so easily, and now you must learn
to ask for it back.
It's not so terrible;
it's like the piano lessons you love
and hate. You know how you want
the music to sound
but have to practice, half in tears,
without much hope.

Eve of St. Agnes in the High School Gym

The saint's been dead too long;
no young girl keeps her vigil. Not one fasts
or prays tonight, for a vision
of the one she'll marry.

A band plays—too loudly—
popular tunes a few years out-of-date.
Young men emerge from a huddle
of teammates, cheerleaders,
fans. They run onto the court,
howling, slapping hands.

Men just a few years older
stand smoking by the door;
their windbreakers advertise a local bar.
Others sit in the stands,
holding sleepy children;
the women with them look worried and tired.

Snow falls silently,
snaking through the streets,
while in the gym, done up like spring
in a pale yellow skirt
and lavender sweater,
a pretty girl sleepwalks
on high heels. She carries herself
to a boy on the bench
who doesn't look up; and the old men sigh.

When the game is over
they flee on the storm.
The saint sits in heaven,
and if anyone's praying
on this chilly night,
let it be for love.

Young Lovers with Pizza

The curve of a smile,
of buttocks;
clothes everywhere,
pizza in a box, laughter
when the telephone intrudes
and you must untangle
legs, breasts, hips
to answer it.
It becomes
a private joke:
the person on the other end
doesn't know a thing.

I envy you,
couples in this town,
in the world:
that first touch, growing,
the dry, breathy heat
and kisses like cool water,
couples lost for a moment
inside each other, inside out.

Don't think of me,
or your duty to God
and telephone. This is silence,
holy and lucky:
a man's hard body
coming soft to the touch, the giddy
generosity
of a woman's breasts, as
light curves gently
around the spinning earth,
around your smiles and
naked hips, holding
everything you need.

Cinderella in Kalamazoo

—*The Medieval Institute, 1990*

Unaccustomed to rain, hills,
trees overhead
gentle as a lover's hands,
I pass the student center, where
medievalists crowd the cash bar,
pause on the steep path
to the dorm, remove my shoes
and am carried for a time
on waters deep as liturgy,
rain sifting through trees
like unexplained tears.
Compline has ended: Cistercians observing
Bernard of Clairvaux's nine-hundredth year
sang the "Salve Regina"
to a perfect, oceanic stillness.

Six-foot-two
and built like a barrel,
the hem of his habit rolling
like waves onto shore, my unlikely fairy godmother
bade me sing. "This is not
a spectator sport," he boomed, inviting me
to learn the chant. And as I joined the others
on the wild green ride
our song became conveyance,
a glorious means of passage
along a narrow road.

"Can you help me?" asks a monk at the door.
Midnight strikes
as we move a table into place
for morning Mass.

I'll be gone by then, on a flight
to the known world, back
through two time zones, my shoes
still soggy, to my drought-stricken plain;
back to my life, the man I love.
I will find it changed,
a dusty old house
where doors no longer fit their frames.

Hope in Elizabeth

From the train
it's a city of roses
and rose keepers,
bald men in spectacles
and torn shirts.
There are miles of roses
in Elizabeth, New Jersey,

backyard arbors
shadowed by refineries
and the turnpike,
jungles of scrap,
still brown water, and poisoned marsh.

None of this matters
to the rose keepers of Elizabeth.
From the backyards of row houses
they bring forth pink roses, yellow roses
and around a house on its own
green plot, a hedge of roses, in red and white.

Surely faith and charity
are fine, but the greatest of these
is roses.

GIVEAWAY

I

In the desert
dryness promotes the formation
of flower buds. This is not aesthetics,
but survival.

In the cancer ward, we laugh.
Solemnly attentive as a deacon
at Mass, a nurse prepares an enema.

Serena tells stories: Mrs. Long-Nose,
a childhood invention,
who moved by farting
in her voluminous skirts. The nurse laughs, too.

II

There is flame
at the center,
gold center
of each bud.
Sometimes we see it,
when blooms are spent.

For three nights I have been sleeping
in Serena's star quilt,
wrapped in a daughter's song of needle and thread,
a song the color of parched grass.

III

Joy at the heart of things:
Serena in the home, sightless at last,
asks to sit by the window
so she can watch the moon rise.

Serena with her daughter,
spending the last money
on bingo, and blankets for the funeral giveaway.

"Did you have fun?" a nurse asked.
"As much fun as you can have," Serena replied,
"playing bingo when you're blind."

The Ignominy of the Living

—Elizabeth Kray, 1916-1987

The undertaker had placed pink netting
around your face. I removed it
and gave you a small bouquet, encumbering you
into eternity."Impedimenta," I hear you say,
scornfully, the way you said it at Penn Station
when we struggled to put your bag onto a contraption
of cords and wheels. "Laurel and Hardy got paid for this,"
I said, the third time it fell off,
narrowly missing my foot.

You would have laughed
at the place we brought you to,
the hush of carpet,
violins sliding through "The Way We Were."
"Please turn the music off," I said, civilly,
to the undertaker's assistant.
We had an open grave—no artificial turf—
and your friends lowered you into the ground.

Once you dreamed your mother sweeping
an earthen floor
in a dark, low-ceilinged room.
I see her now. I, too, want to run.
And "the ignominy of the living,"
words you nearly spat out
when one of your beloved dead
was ill-remembered; I thought of that
as I removed the netting.

Today I passed St. Mary's
as the Angelus sounded.
You would have liked that,
the ancient practice
in a prairie town not a hundred years old,
the world careering disastrously toward the twenty-first century.
Then a recording of "My Way" came scratching out
on the electronic carillon.
"Oh, hell," I said,
and prayed for Frank Sinatra, too.

Vision: A Note on Astrophysics

—for Miriam Schmitt, O.S.B.

Learned men
of the twentieth century, armed with large
finite numbers and radiotelescopes
as big as football fields to measure the pulse of light
from stars beyond the range
of human vision, conclude that this world,
all we call nature,
was once inside such a star.
Heisenberg shrugs
and says, "I am not sure
what an electron is,
but it's something like a cloud of possibilities."

Hildegard
saw it plain,
in the monastery at Rupertsberg,
midway through her life, in 1140 or so:
Eve
as a cloud,
leaf-green, shining,
containing stars . . .

THE UNCERTAINTY PRINCIPLE

—for Robert West, O.S.B.

We change it
by looking: what's moving in the heart
or the farthest star,
and when people are true believers
we may know of the mystery
how it works,
or if it does,
but not the two together.

Here at the abbey
bells confide the hour.
A scientist could tell
how crude
a means, how inexact
they are.
Time does not move,
the sky is not blue—the end
of the spectrum
and beginning of light—
it is all in us,
breathed in, let go.

Monks shift in their choir:
stomachs, and the old floor
groan through the homily.
Here in the heart,
where the hours keep,
we are learning eternity
every step of the way.

LAND OF THE LIVING

Menstruation is primitive,
no getting around that fact, as
I wipe my blood from the floor
at 3 A.M. in the monastery guest room,
alone in this community
of sleeping men.

Once again, I have given up
the having of children,
and celebrate instead
a monthly flowering
of the not-to-be,
and let it go without regret.

Earlier tonight, a young monk, laughing,
splashed my face
with holy water. Then, just as unexpectedly,
he flew down a banister, and
for one millisecond
was an angel—robed,
without feet—
all irrepressible joy
and good news.

The black madonna watched us,
expectant as earth just plowed.

My sister holds her baby
in a photograph. They smile at me
from the mirror I've placed them on.
Lili sits like the Christ Child
on her mother's lap. She sits very straight
in a blood-red dress
and stares into something
that makes her look amused, and wise.

It's here, in the land of the living,
the psalm says we shall see God's goodness.
I'm glad to be here,
a useless woman,
sleepless and kept waiting,
as breath keeps coming,
as the blood flows.

Ascension

Why do you stand looking up at the sky?—Acts 1:11

It wasn't just wind chasing
thin, gunmetal clouds
across a loud sky;
it wasn't the feeling that one might ascend
on that excited air,
rising like a trumpet note,

and it wasn't just my sister's water breaking,
her crying out,
the downward draw of blood and bone . . .

It was all of that,
mud and new grass
pushing up through melting snow,
the lilac in bud by my front door
bent low
by last week's ice storm.

Now the new mother, that leaky vessel,
begins to nurse her child,
beginning the long good-bye.

A. J.'s Passage

Poor baby, hold on;
poor, sleepy baby, passed into my arms.
We are passing into hell; hold on.
We renounce the forces of evil
and you cry out.

Poor, sleepy baby
wanting nothing more than the food
your mother has become
for you, wanting to go into
this night at her breast.

Brilliance
catches your eye,
the candle
in your mother's hand, her hair
a halo, your fingers transparent.

Poor baby, our words wash over you
and you brush them away.
You want the candle now,
and you want your mother.
It is not yet time
to follow her into the dark.

Poor little baby:
water on your hair,
chrism on your forehead,
dried milk on your chin.
Poor brave little baby; hold on.

EPIPHANY

—Vladimir Ussachevsky, 1911-1990

The night you died
you rushed into the apartment
where I was sorting your papers,
weary as the girl
who has until sunrise
to spin straw into gold.
In a disreputable black raincoat,
well-traveled,
you were your old-world,
courtly self,
despite the haste, the fuss
of leaving.

From deep in your pockets
you drew out coins, ticket stubs,
a black-and-white photograph
of the Orthodox Church in Manchuria
where you first learned liturgy, the ebb and flow
of choirs. More than sixty years
have passed: your first friends
on earth, dogs and birds
and tumbleweeds from the fields around Hailar
run silent as shadows through Calvary Hospice
in the Bronx, time and space
unraveling, dark threads at your hem.

Now my sister's baby wakes
in Honolulu, weaving his hands in air.
He hears the birds
and answers them,
calling to the light.

THE MONASTERY ORCHARD IN EARLY SPRING

God's cows are in the fields,
safely grazing. I can see them
through bare branches,
through the steady rain.
Fir trees seem ashamed
and tired, bending under winter coats.

I, too, want to be light enough
for this day: throw off impediments,
push like a tulip
through a muddy smear of snow,

I want to take the rain to heart
and feel it move
like possibility, the idea
of change, through things
seen and unseen,
forces, principalities, powers.

Newton named the force that pulls the apple
and the moon with it,
toward the center of the earth.
Augustine found a desire as strong: to steal,
to possess, then throw away.
Encounter with fruit is dangerous:
the pear's womanly shape forever mocked him.

A man and a woman are talking.
Rain moves down and
branches lift up
to learn again
how to hold their fill of green
and blossom, and bear each fruit to glory,
letting it fall.

The Word Itself: A Love Poem

In the fruit
is the power of return:
one slippery, ruby seed
bound Persephone to Hades
and a child I know, on his first
day of school, held fast to an apple
his mother had given him,
sure that if he ate it
he would not ever see her again.

In the fruit
is seed,
binding mother and child,

and in the fruit the flower,
generation,
seed and spore,

all that lets itself be taken
to make what it can
of wind and water, earth and light,
the here and now.

You are empty
with grief, and shall be filled
with consolation. To you I seem
a plenitude; I shall be emptied

and in the word itself,
(the ripened ovary
in edible, sweet, and fleshy
form) find my own mother's breast
again. Childless,
both of us,
useless
in this season (my motherhood
hidden
where only God
can find it,
or the voice of love)
we must use what we can
of riotous spring.

How fair and pleasant you are.
How fragrant attraction,
all conversation;
how sure
our tongues,
each fresh remark,
each mellowing silence.

Come—soon—
come, taste the fruit
of the word itself, sprung up
and opened wide,
that progeny of joy.

A Letter to Paul Carroll, Who Said I Must Become a Catholic so That I Can Pray for Him

It's here, in the silent monastery corridor,
I think of you and say a prayer
for those lost by the way,
for the foolish virgins,
not the wise. It's your prayer, too, Paul,
for the losers
of eternal life, the unfaithful
departed, who sit alone
in the near-dark, writing,
Why—do they shut Me out of Heaven?

You and I know that now
Miss Dickinson descends a staircase
in the Elysian Fields. With her is
Miss Thérèse of Lisieux,
who said to Jesus,
I am happy not enjoying the sight of that beautiful heaven
here on earth, as long as you open it in eternity
for unbelievers. Here, Paul, where they pray
and cross themselves
and tend bees and run a print shop
and farm and come to choir
stinking of sweat. They're Catholic enough
even for you, and their prayers rise like incense
carried by the angels up to God.
Of course I believe it. Even the Methodist
in me believes in the change,
the bread and wine that turns into Benedictines
dressed like ravens
who reappear each morning
to pray and sing.

Of course I don't belong.
In habits as black as unbelief, as black
as the Black Madonna,
who answers all prayers from the heart,
they take me in out of charity.

When I'm among them
I say all the "Glorias"
and "Alleluias" and "Amens,"
and often I really mean it.
I don't know what I'm saying,
Paul, and that's the point.

"THE SKY IS FULL OF BLUE AND FULL OF THE MIND OF GOD"

a girl wrote once,
in winter, in a school
at Minot Air Force Base.
A girl tall for her age,
with cornrows and a shy, gap-toothed smile.
She was lonely in North Dakota,
for God, for trees,
warm weather, the soft cadences of Louisiana.
I think of her as the sky stretches tight
all around.

I'm at the Conoco on I-94, waiting for the eastbound bus.
Mass is not over; the towers of the monastery
give no sign
that deep in the church
men in robes and chasubles
are playing at a serious game.

I feel like dancing on this
wooden porch: "Gotta get to you, baby,
been runnin' all over town."
The jukebox is wired to be heard outside
and I dance to keep warm,
my breath carried white on the breeze.

The sky stretches tight, a mandorla of cloud
around the sun. And now
Roy Orbison reaches for the stratosphere:
something about a blue angel.
It is the Sanctus; I know it; I'm ready.

The Blue Light

The angels stood
with their backs to me.
I was six months old
and dying.
I had no name for them,
for anything.
They were cold,
not like my mother.

Just beyond the angels
was a blue light
and like any child
I reached for it
because it was pretty.
I wanted to curl my fingers around it
and hold on.

The angels didn't move,
but the blue light receded.
Children are easily disappointed,
and I wanted it so much.

I lay in the hospital crib, angry,
rolling my head
and crying. It may have been one of the angels
who picked me up
and returned me to my mother;
I don't know. But I knew my parents
were as helpless as I.

I learned it too soon.

II

I learned to keep moving,
back through the pain.
I had no word for it.

And the nurse who fed me a bottle
through the operation,
the doctors working helplessly
with all their skill;
it was their world
I learned to want.

The love that moved me then
still moves me. I saw the perfect
backs of angels
singed with light:

I turned from them,
I let them go.

How I Came to Drink
My Grandmother's Piano

It has to do with giving,
and with letting go,
with how the earth rotates
on its axis
to make an oblate spheroid.

It has to do
with how it all comes round.

There was a piano
in my grandmother's house.
I inherited it,
but never learned to play.
I used it as a bookshelf
and dust collector
and finally gave it to a church up the street.

I was snowed in at a trailer house
in Regent, North Dakota,
when Rita offered me a glass
of dandelion wine.
"That's some glass," I said,
much too fancy for our thrown-together meal
of hamburgers and fried potatoes.
"Yes, isn't it?" she replied,
fingering the cut glass pattern.
"A friend gave it to me.
Someone had given it to her,
but she never used it."

I began to hear that piano
as Rita poured the wine.
The dandelions spun around:
glad to be yellow again,
glad to be free of the dark.

THE COMPANIONABLE DARK

of here and now,
seed lying dormant
in the earth. The dark
to which all lost things come—scarves
and rings and precious photographs, and
of course, our beloved
dead. The brooding dark,
our most vulnerable hours, limbs loose
in sleep, mouths agape.
The faithful dark,
where each door leads,
each one of us, alone.
The dark of God come close
as breath, our one companion
all the way through, the dark
of a needle's eye.

Not the easy dark
of dusk and candles,
but dark from which comforts flee.
The deep down dark
of one by one,
dark of wind
and dust, dark in which stars burn.
The floodwater dark
of hope, Jesus in agony
in the garden, Esther pacing
her bitter palace. A dark
by which we see, dark like truth,
like flesh on bone:
Help me, who am alone,
and have no help but thee.

WHAT SONG, THEN?

When my life is alien soil
and a wind
like fear
makes restless ground
of all I have done—

what song, then,
to send out roots
that will drink the rain
that does not come—

how could I sing?

Watch light come
from dark and mist rise
from waters
as sky and shore
emerge out of night,
and a tree half-green,
half-bare.

Half-afraid of what is in me
(though God has called it good)
I sob over nothing,

desires I cannot name.

Sing us, they say,
a song you remember . . .

ALL SAINTS, ALL SOULS

—*William Stafford, 1914–1993*

I had disappeared
into grassland, the high plateau
where the Missouri begins
to claw its way south, where hail
wets the wreckage of fields. I accept it
gratefully, even this
bitter pill.

The chaos of the wind
had taken me, like topsoil
off a hill, dark steam
churning, away
from earth. But you kept me
on your radar, Bill—*Kneel down,*
you said, *explore*
for the poem.

I love the saints,
Thérèse cried in mortal illness—*I love the saints,*
they want to see—the other side
of death's bitter
remedy, Bill,
the sleep
of grass, both root
and blaze, the river ice waiting
as time forms its word, the garden
where we need not hide.

Home, you say,
as the feasts wheel round

in the dark of the year, All Saints,
All Souls; all song
and story. Sing it now, Bill,
let it come.

A DEATH IN ADVENT

I hope they were kind,
Jerry, the orderlies
and nurses who laughed,
despite themselves—even
in intensive care, they say,
you were a funny man.

I hope you heard
a human voice
above the clatter of Code Blue,
your dear, enlarged heart
giving out late
in the afternoon
on the feast of St. Andrew, a man
who died, as Christ did,
on a cross—
people were not kind, then,
except for a thief
who asked for Paradise.

They say
you looked haunted,
Jerry, the gaunt look of men
too long in hospital
or jail, having glimpsed the world
gratuitous with mercy,
honed to specks of dust.
Mercy, how it goes on.
How old we become
with waiting—at thirty-seven,
Jerry, I hoped maybe you had
half a chance—how we forget

what to ask for, poor fools
among the living, with the old jokes
still the best:
The check is in the mail.
Behold, I am coming soon.

A Litany for Basil, on Leaving Oz

I don't know how to do it,
but I see the plains before me
like a book.
I don't know why pain comes
in waves, but I see
grass in wind.
I don't know how it happens
but I listen to the story.
I don't know why
it takes so long,
but I love to hear it.
I don't know how
the days will run,
but I long to see them unfold.
I don't know why
it's in us: this love that moves
in color, through fears
that are black and white.

"You've always had the power,"
the good witch says. Why love is like death,
only longer. Amen. Amen.

Mysteries of the Incarnation

I. "She Said Yeah"

The land lies open: summer fallow, hayfield, pasture. Folds of
cloud mirror buttes knife-edged in shadow. One monk smears
honey on his toast, another peels an orange.

A bell rings three times, as the Angelus begins, bringing to
mind Gabriel and Mary. "She said yeah," the Rolling Stones
sing from a car on the interstate, "She said yeah." And the bells
pick it up, many bells now, saying it to Mechtild, the barn cat,
pregnant again; to Ephrem's bluebirds down the draw; to the
grazing cattle and the monks (virgins, some of them) eating
silently before the sexy tongue of a hibiscus blossom at their
refectory window. "She said yeah." And then the angel left her.

II. Imperatives

Look at the birds
Consider the lilies
Drink ye all of it

Ask
Seek
Knock
Enter by the narrow gate

Do not be anxious
Judge not; do not give dogs what is holy

Go: be it done for you
Do not be afraid
Maiden, arise
Young man, I say, arise

Stretch out your hand
Stand up, be still
Rise, let us be going . . .

Love
Forgive
Remember me

> *And a great portent appeared in the sky: a woman*
> *clothed with the sun, with the moon under her feet,*
> *and on her head a crown of twelve stars; she was with child.*
> —Revelation 12:1

Loons, antiphonal,
call from lake to riverine.
"You know," he said, moon
rising full, or nearly so, "this is more
than just us two." It is a path
newly forming
to the Virgin's little house—a "princess
house," a child had called it—as if
we could walk there, to Stella Maris
Chapel, though the woods are dark,
the moat a dragon's tail. Darling,
it is full-to-bursting, as big as the starstuff
of which we're made. That is why
the dragon waits.

Monks,
antiphonal, call across
the abbey church, husbanding the song
within, this longing
to be human, as the loon is a loon.
The sun makes a path
that blinds us, clothes us
painfully, in light: a man
and a woman, asking,
"How did we get here?"

"How long is the road?"
However it ends,
it begins with us, this feast
by which we come to see
how beautiful we are.

IV. The Throne of Grace

First their car broke down, then Darlene and Kaylee drank up all the butterscotch schnapps in Newcastle, Wyoming. That night they had a chew in the motel hot tub, on the theory that chlorine, heat, and nicotine would steam the alcohol out. "I had to wear my sweat suit," Darlene explained, "and in the morning it was still soaking wet. I had a pair of jeans, but nothing for on top. I figured I could wear my jacket if I remembered to keep it zipped." But when she and Kaylee went across Main Street for breakfast and Kaylee took her jacket off, Darlene forgot and did the same. "I'm standing there in my bra at seven in the morning," she said, "and this one old coot looked up from his bowl of cereal, his face lit up like a kid on Christmas morning. Then he shook his head and went back to eating."

V. True love

binds all wounds,
wounds all heels,
whatever. You can tell.
William Buckley,
Gore Vidal, Sampson
and Delilah. Paul
and the Corinthians.
You can tell.

It makes us fight
and bleed, takes us to the heights,
the deeps, where we don't
want to go. Adam and Eve, Noah
and Mrs., David,
Bathsheba. Ruth,
Naomi. You can tell.

The way light surges
out of nothing. The Magdalene,
the gardener. God help us,
we are God's chosen now.

Taking the Blue

Trees gossip
in the ghost-light. Early stars
climb the sky
and a breeze descends,
touching my arm
lightly, like my grandmother
at the last. I climb the hill
at the edge of town as
dust devils rise in the fields.

What is it for, any of it,
choosing to live
day in, day out,
in a parched land?

My grandmother's prayer, "Keep me friendly
to myself," has weathered badly
in the long crescendo
of Romans 8. Her handwriting fades
on the yellowed page and I have failed to love
the river in the tree,
the stream in the grass,
the ocean of blood
that moves in us. I am,
inexplicably, here
and now, already taking
the next breath.

Trees gossip; dark moves
like the ocean this land
once was: stubble, grass, ground,
turning in the last light
gold, green, blue.

CHILDREN OF DIVORCE

"We should imagine that we are in heaven,"
I read, as the pilot announces a holding pattern.
Two children of divorce
are busy with the game of "Doorbell."
"Who's there?" they scream
every time
a bell sounds; they pretend to look for faces
in the storm clouds.
The stewardess has seated them together,
a boy and a girl,

pretending not to be afraid.
"We should imagine that we are in heaven,"
insists Theodore of Mopsuestia, a name
the children would adore, no doubt
a close relation of Mopsy
Cottontail. The world robes itself
in ribbons of light, each inundated place on earth
a shiny coin, a medium of exchange
in the brooding dark through which we pass.
The girl asks, "Can a tornado pick up a plane and throw it?"
The boy says, "I can't look, it's too scary,"

as he pulls down the window shade.
"It's an ocean down there,"
says the girl, "we'll be lost at sea."
"It's too scary," the boy says again,
lifting the shade
as the pilot announces our approach for landing
in Minneapolis. Theodore
and the girl are right:
it doesn't look like any world we know.

"We're gonna die," says the girl.
"I can't look," says the boy, "we're not gonna make it."
"Oh, is that the city—aren't the lights pretty?"
"We're not gonna make it."
The great river shines in the newly minted dusk—pale and black; red, white—"He'll never make the runway," says the boy, "we're gonna die." "Oh," says the girl, "just look at the lights."

ANNIVERSARY

Suddenly, Michael, a prince of the angels, came to my
aid. Suddenly, Gabriel flew down and touched me, and
I understood. And the Lord sent Raphael to heal Tobias
and Sarah.—LITURGY OF THE HOURS FOR THE FEAST OF
MICHAEL AND ALL ANGELS

It touched my shoulder,
and bid me stand. It touched my lips
like a lover, that I might speak.
Around me was Babel, confusion of tongues.
The angel held a mirror to it,
and Pentecost flamed. I heard a word,
and understood ten thousand.
It said what angels always say,
"Do not be afraid."

I prayed for my love, who is far away,
and as the prayer winged up—the prayer
of our life,
and fear for the rest of it—
as it became too dark, too glorious
for me to see, the angel took it
down and through, over and above, wherever
it is that angels go.

"Will you live with me?" I asked,
before I knew the word for love,
on Madison Avenue, by a ginkgo tree growing
through a sidewalk grate. "Will you love me?"
you ask, after all these years.
Let me not understand, but do it.

FOGGY

Jeremiah shouts, "Break up
your fallow ground!" and as
I take my spade in hand, as far
as I can see, great clods of earth
are waiting, heavy and dark,
a hopeless task. First weeds will come,
then whatever it is
I've planted. I feel the struggle
in my knees and back.

All I can see
is close at hand,
monks who have
slouched, shuffled, stumbled, strutted,
and sauntered into church
this morning,
as they did yesterday,
and will again tomorrow.
Isn't that something? I say
to myself. I have no idea what,

except that it's happiness, pure
and simple, and questions fade
as great clouds
descend, as furrows
reel beneath my step: no *what,* or *how,* or
where is your God?
Only *return, come back,*
cleanse your hearts.

The Tolling

Walking uphill
in the great womb of dawn,
words of Thérèse come to me,
. . . *my little story, which was like a fairy tale,*
has turned into prayer. And people must
have puddings, Emily Dickinson chimes in,
with the same tone of wonder, into
the jumble of my mind.

Climbing the long hill
to church, I wonder
at the coming of the light,
how dusk after vespers
was the same, beyond purple
or blue, a sky
that made me sing.
Easter, 1896: bit by bit,
Thérèse coughed out
her lungs and faith
turned dark, *my faith*
that Dark adores, Emily
whispers, more solemn now.

Orion stands watch above the bell tower.
I enter and take a seat in the monks' choir.
Our hymn says life is borrowed;
"Let us pray for Brother Louis," says the prayer leader,
and after, a monk appears like an angel
of the resurrection, to show me hymns
that Louis wrote—years ago,
now—the poetry clean
and spare—and to tell the story: how the plague

touched his heart, and Louis went to Minneapolis
to care for AIDS patients. How his heart
gave out and he had to come home,
how long he suffered.

Louis's poetry still makes us sing—
the hospice is in others' hands.
Young monks will carry him into church
through the baptistry, where it all began.
They will bury him up the hill.

I sit out the tolling
in the Mary chapel;
carved eight hundred years ago
by hands of faith,
she sits very still, with my friend Clellie's face,
the face of any mother.
Tears come, not for Louis,
whom I never knew. And it is not
the tolling, insistent as death.
It is not the length of it—*how long
will it go on—I have things to do, I'm hungry,
morning goes so fast—*
not the tolling, but the silence after.

Hide and Seek

Your true and only Son is love.
—Louis Blenkner, O.S.B., Te Deum

A thunderclap
rakes the field of sleep—must be
the consecration, enough
to wake the dead—lightning
so soon after, Brother John saw it
arc through the church. We
said good-bye to Louis, and rains came at
the Agnus Dei, our need for tears
answered by the elements. I get up
to close the window and remember:
Wichita, 3:09 A.M.
by the light
of the alarm, a hotel room
facing east. The city skyline
jumps with each bolt, playing
hide and seek.

Hide and seek: Maria
in the baptistry on her second
birthday, running around the granite font;
that night, Louis's coffin
carried in, and blessed there.
Hide and seek: the saints
in light, who have died
and live—Louis's
words to me, though we never met—
that helped me live through an evil time.

I know
the grubby strivings
for each syllable, the search after words
that bolt and run. Louis,
I give thanks for you, for
all that drove you to it.
I give thanks
for the way
it all goes on, thunder and lightning,
the message
and the messenger, great
bone-white wings
that part the eastern sky
as we carry you to your grave. For folds of earth
that admit us all—and a crescent
of blue light I never saw—for unsearchable riches
that reach into our lives, love
calling us by name.

EMILY IN CHOIR

Emily holds her father's hand;
she dances in place
through the Invitatory,
and refuses the book with no pictures.
"This is boring," she whispers
in the silence between psalms.

Candles lit in honor of the guardian angels
make rivers of air that bend the stone
walls of the abbey church. "Why are the men
wearing costumes?" Emily asks.
"They're the brothers,"
her father explains, and Emily says, "Well!
They must have a very strict mother!"

The Grave is strict, says another Emily;
Emily-here-and-now plays with the three
shadows her hands make
on the open page. *While the clergyman
tells Father and Vinnie that "this Corruptible
shall put on Incorruption," it has already done so
and they go defrauded.*

Brimful of knowledge, Emily shakes my arm:
"They're the monks," she says,
"the men who sing," and she runs
up the aisle, out into the day,
to *where the angels are . . .*

*In the name of the Bee—
And of the Butterfly—
And of the Breeze—Amen!*

NOTES

"Kitchen Trinity"; *The Holy Trinity,* icon painted by Andrew Rublev in 1425.

"My Favorite Woman in the World"; Story is from Rebecca West, *Black Lamb and Grey Falcon.*

"In Praise of Darkness"; Allusion in lines 24-26 is from Psalm 19.

"St. Mary of Egypt Speaks . . . "; St. Mary of Egypt (5th c). A teenaged runaway, she became a prostitute in Alexandria. At the age of thirty she experienced a religious conversion on a pilgrimage to Jerusalem and spent the rest of her life as a hermit in the desert.

"The Age of Reason"; Epigram is a paraphrase of a remark Picasso made to Douglas Duncan.

"Vision"; Contains a paraphrase of a remark physicist Werner Heisenberg once made to an interviewer.

"Land of the Living"; Allusion in line 33 is from Psalm 27.

"The Uncertainty Principle"; Discovered by Werner Heisenberg in the 1920s, the Uncertainty Principle, proves that at the subatomic level the act of observation changes the speed and/or the location of whatever is observed.

"A Letter to Paul Carroll"; Quotes are from Emily Dickinson (1830–1886), Poem #248, and from the autobiography of St. Thérèse of Lisieux (1873–1897), *Story of a Soul.*

"The Sky is Full of Blue . . . "; "The mandorla is an iconographic symbol in the shape of a circle or an oval signifying heaven, Divine Glory, light . . . most often differing shades of blue." Leonid Ouspensky, *The Meaning of Icons.*

"The companionable dark"; Title alludes to Psalm 88; quote is from the Book of Esther 4 C:14.

"A Death in Advent"; Quote in last line is from Rev. 22:20.

"All Saints, All Souls"; Quotes are from William Stafford, *You Must Revise Your Life,* and Thérèse of Lisieux, *Last Conversations.*

"Foggy"; First line is from Jer. 4:3.

"Children of Divorce"; Theodore of Mopsuestia (dates 392–428??), theologian of the early Christian church. Quote is taken from baptismal homily #15.

"The Tolling"; Quotes are from Thérèse of Lisieux (*Story of a Soul*), Thomas Higginson's account of Emily Dickinson at their meeting in August 1870, and Emily Dickinson, Poem #7.

"Emily in Choir"; An Invitatory is a psalm sung at the beginning of a prayer service. Quotes are from Emily Dickinson: Poem #408, Letter #508 (1873), and Poem #18.

ACKNOWLEDGMENTS

The author and publisher wish to acknowledge the following publications in which some of these poems first appeared: *AGNI* ("Physics Defeats Me," "Thinking About Louise Bogan"); *Aluminum Canoe* ("A Litany for Basil"); *Chicago Review* ("A Letter to Paul Carroll," "Pommes de Terre"); *Elkhorn Review* ("Persephone"); *5 A.M.* ("Eve of St. Agnes in the High School Gym," "Land of the Living," "Young Lovers with Pizza"); *Journal of Feminist Studies in Religion* ("In Praise of Darkness"); *Literary Review* ("Hope in Elizabeth"); *North Dakota Quarterly* ("The Wine"); *Northern Lights* ("The Throne of Grace"); *Paris Review* ("A Prayer to Eve"); *Parnassus: Poetry in Review* ("The Blue Light," "For My Aunt Mary," "Hester Prynne Recalls a Sunday in June"); *Plainswoman* ("Little Girls in Church," "Perennials"); *Poetry* ("Ascension"); *Prairie Schooner* ("How I Came to Drink My Grandmother's Piano," "The sky is full of blue and full of the mind of God," "The Wedding in the Courthouse"); *River Oak Review* ("The Age of Reason"); *Salmagundi* ("My Favorite Woman in the World"); *Sisters Today* ("The Uncertainty Principle," "Vision: A Note on Astrophysics"); *Virginia Quarterly Review* ("A. J.'s Passage," "Epiphany," "Housecleaning," "Kitchen Trinity," "She Said Yeah'"); and *Witness* ("LaVonne's Mantlepiece," "St. Mary of Egypt").

"The Ignominy of the Living" and "Giveaway" originally appeared in *The New Yorker.*

Several poems have appeared in chapbooks: *"How I Came to Drink My Grandmother's Piano,"* Benet Biscop Press, Blue Cloud Abbey, 1989. *"All Saints, All Souls,"* (with drawings by Ed Colker) Philadelphia: Borowsky Center for Publishing Arts, University of the Arts/ Haybarn Press, 1993. *"The Astronomy of Love"* (with drawings by Ed Colker), Mt. Kisco, N.Y.: Haybarn Press, 1994. "'She Said Yeah'" was published as a broadside by the Institute for Regional Studies, Fargo, North Dakota, 1993.

My gratitude to the Poetry Society of America for awarding "A Prayer to Eve" the Mary Carolyn Davies Award in 1989, and to the Bush Foundation and the John Simon Guggenheim Memorial Foundation for financial support. A special thanks to the Institute for Ecumenical and Cultural Research of Collegeville, Minnesota, and to my Benedictine, Cistercian, and Dominican friends for their nourishing hospitality.

Kathleen Norris 

is a freelance writer. She is the author of *Dakota: A Spiritual Geography* and several collections of poetry. She lives in western South Dakota with her husband, the poet David Dwyer.

PITT POETRY SERIES

ED OCHESTER, GENERAL EDITOR

Claribel Alegría, *Flowers from the Volcano*
Claribel Alegría, *Woman of the River*
Debra Allbery, *Walking Distance*
Maggie Anderson, *Cold Comfort*
Maggie Anderson, *A Space Filled with Moving*
Robin Becker, *Giacometti's Dog*
Siv Cedering, *Letters from the Floating World*
Lorna Dee Cervantes, *Emplumada*
Robert Coles, *A Festering Sweetness: Poems of
     American People*
Nancy Vieira Couto, *The Face in the Water*
Jim Daniels, *M-80*
Kate Daniels, *The Niobe Poems*
Kate Daniels, *The White Wave*
Toi Derricotte, *Captivity*
Sharon Doubiago, *South America Mi Hija*
Stuart Dybek, *Brass Knuckles*
Odysseus Elytis, *The Axion Esti*
Jane Flanders, *Timepiece*
Forrest Gander, *Lynchburg*
Richard Garcia, *The Flying Garcias*
Suzanne Gardinier, *The New World*
Gary Gildner, *Blue Like the Heavens: New & Selected Poems*
Elton Glaser, *Color Photographs of the Ruins*
Hunt Hawkins, *The Domestic Life*
Lawrence Joseph, *Curriculum Vitae*
Lawrence Joseph, *Shouting at No One*
Julia Kasdorf, *Sleeping Preacher*
Etheridge Knight, *The Essential Etheridge Knight*
Bill Knott, *Poems, 1963–1988*
Ted Kooser, *One World at a Time*
Ted Kooser, *Sure Signs: New and Selected Poems*
Ted Kooser, *Weather Central*
Larry Levis, *The Widening Spell of the Leaves*
Larry Levis, *Winter Stars*
Larry Levis, *Wrecking Crew*
Walter McDonald, *Counting Survivors*
Irene McKinney, *Six O'Clock Mine Report*
Archibald MacLeish, *The Great American Fourth
     of July Parade*
Peter Meinke, *Liquid Paper: New and Selected Poems*